LLC & S Corporation Essentials

Your Ultimate FAQ Guide for Entrepreneurs

MADE SIMPLE

Your Top 26 Questions About LLCs and

S Corporations Answered

Dr. Rosie Milligan

Published And Distributed By
Professional Publishing House
1425 W. Manchester Ave. Ste B
Los Angeles, California 90047
323-750-3592
Email: professionalpublishinghouse@yahoo.com
www.Professionalpublishinghouse.com

Cover design: TWA Solutions
First printing June 2024
978-1-7328982-6-4
10 9 8 7 6 5 4 3 2 1

Disclaimer:

This comprehensive guide serves to augment the foundational knowledge vital for aspiring entrepreneurs venturing into establishing an LLC or S Corporation enterprise. This manual does not replace the need for professional legal counsel.

I strongly urge you to engage the expertise of a qualified attorney to address any legal intricacies pertinent to your business endeavors and to obtain the services of a certified tax accountant for tailored tax counsel specific to your business operations.

I am not a certified attorney or tax professional. However, with decades of firsthand experience as the owner of several successful businesses, a seasoned senior estate planner, business consultant, and business coach, I have led many thriving ventures and helped countless individuals navigate the complexities of entrepreneurship. I offer insights and strategies to empower your entrepreneurial journey.

Acknowledgments and Dedications

I want to acknowledge the trailblazing businesspeople who came before me. Your journey from humble beginnings to remarkable achievements has paved the way for countless others, including myself. Your examples of resilience and innovation have been a constant source of inspiration.

I dedicate this book to every entrepreneur, regardless of the level of success you have achieved. Your determination to carve out your own path is commendable, and I applaud your courage and perseverance.

I dedicate the book to my youngest son and business sidekick, Cedric Andrea Milligan, Sr. Your unwavering support during our travels and dedication to maintaining the business in my absence is invaluable. Your inspiration ignited my passion for educating aspiring entrepreneurs about the benefits of choosing the LLC business entity. Thank you for being my rock and driving force on this incredible journey.

A heartfelt thank you to my children: Pamela Milligan-McGee, M.D., John Sherman Milligan, Jr., and Cedric Andrea Milligan, Sr. Your unwavering encouragement and support has been invaluable. Your cooperation allowed me to travel the country for lectures and book signings with peace of mind, knowing you were taking care of everything at home. This book is as much a testament to your support as it is to my efforts.

About Dr. Rosie Milligan

Dr. Rosie Milligan, a woman who knows no limits, is a prominent figure in the business and financial world, known for her multifaceted roles and exceptional expertise. As the CEO of Professional Business Management & Consulting Services and the Founder of My Tech Academy, she has established herself as one of Los Angeles's renowned financial gurus. Her extensive background includes being a seasoned senior estate planner, business coach, business consultant, and holder of a Ph.D. in Business Administration. Her motto: "Erase 'NO,' Step Over 'CAN'T,' and Move Forward With Life" has been a motivating influence for hundreds to whom she has been a mentor and role model.

Dr. Milligan's reputation extends nationwide, with individuals and organizations seeking her out for top-tier business and financial coaching services. With over twenty-six authored books and four hundred fifty books published for other authors, she owns the largest and most prominent African American publishing house in the nation. In addition, she hosts a weekly talk show that further solidifies her influence and reach.

Dr. Milligan's approach revolves around imparting expert guidance to bid farewell to mediocrity. Leveraging her impressive educational achievements, a wealth of business experiences, and years spent consulting non-profit organizations, startups, and established businesses, she offers membership packages that incorporate her personalized coaching methods and proven, effective business strategies. This combination has consistently produced tangible results, ensuring a pathway to a thriving business.

Want to learn more about Dr. Rosie?
Visit her websites:
www.drrosie.com
www.mytechacademy.net

TABLE OF CONTENTS

INTRODUCTION

In today's rapidly evolving business landscape, it's crucial to equip yourself with the knowledge to jumpstart your business and avoid errors that could lead to hardships or failure. As we navigate Artificial Intelligence (AI) and the digital world, the need to fail-proof our businesses are even more critical. As AI advancements continue, experts predict that thousands of corporate jobs will become obsolete, which will make it less viable to rely on returning to these positions as a traditional fallback. Therefore, building resilient businesses is essential not only for personal success but also for creating a financial legacy for future generations. Remember, the more you learn, the more you can earn.

Many entrepreneurs find themselves in business by default. Corporate downsizing, AI-driven job eliminations, and digital transformations have rendered many skills obsolete. As a result, individuals often use severance pay or retirement funds to start their own businesses, despite lacking prior business experience or computer literacy. These new entrepreneurs, who once relied on clerks and secretaries, now face the challenge of managing their businesses without adequate technological skills.

My Tech Academy

The COVID-19 pandemic highlighted the urgent need for technology and business training. It was during this time that I realized the critical necessity for comprehensive support in these areas. In response, I founded My Tech Academy in 2019 to address widespread unemployment and business closures.

During the pandemic, people inundated my office with calls for help with unemployment benefits, SBA loans, and other essential applications. Many people lacked access to computers or the Internet, and those who did often struggled with basic computer skills. I also witnessed countless missed opportunities for business owners unable to access vital PPP loans and grants because of inadequate computer and Internet skills. Their struggle with uploading and downloading essential documents highlighted the need for support in a critical area. Helping them revealed a significant gap in technological proficiency. We had to invite them to our office, adhering to safety protocols, to provide the support—free of charge.

The pandemic exposed the vulnerability of business owners who lacked a web presence and technological savvy. These deficiencies hindered their ability to compete in a global economy and jeopardized their future economic success. This motivated me to launch My Tech Academy (mytechacademy.net), which offers free webinars on AI, a la carte classes on basic computer skills, Internet mastery, AI marketing, business tax compliance, and everything you need to know to start and run an LLC.

CHAPTER 1

Why More People Are Starting Businesses, Particularly LLCs and S Corporations

M any people are starting businesses out of necessity. Corporate downsizing, job relocations, and skill obsolescence have left many with no choice but to venture into entrepreneurship. Self-determination and self-preservation have become significant motivators.

Starting a business not only offers personal wealth generation, it also provides a means to leave a legacy and create generational wealth. The most popular business structures are:

- Sole Proprietorship
- S Corporation
- General Partnerships
- Corporations

However, the Limited Liability Company (LLC) has emerged as the most popular choice among new small businesses in the United States. Over one-third of new small businesses are LLCs.

Benefits of an LLC

One of the main reasons for the popularity of an LLC is the protection it offers. In a litigious society, the potential for business liabilities that could threaten personal assets is a significant concern. An LLC provides limited liability, which means owners are only responsible for business debts up to the value of their shares in the LLC.

An LLC combines the best aspects of partnerships and corporations, offering protection from personal liability while being relatively easy to form and maintain. It enhances business credibility and improves access to credit, as banks are more likely to extend credit to an LLC than to a sole proprietorship or partnership.

An LLC can also choose to be taxed as a corporation, providing flexibility in tax treatment. Additionally, an S Corporation allows the business to sell stock, offering further opportunities for growth and investment.

This manual does not provide exhaustive information on choosing the right business structure. There is much to learn about LLCs, S Corporations, and general business management. For more comprehensive guidance, my sister, Attorney Clara Hunter King, and I have authored *What You Need To Know Before You Start A Business,* which has helped many entrepreneurs across the country.

For those looking to jumpstart their LLC or S Corporation quickly and proficiently, consider enrolling in a webinar at My Tech Academy (mytechacademy.net) and joining the LLC Bootcamp Program.

As a business coach, I also recommend consulting a business coach. Often, business owners are too close to their operations to see the bigger picture. It's essential to work on your business rather than just in it.

CHAPTER 2

Unveiling Answers to the Most Frequently Asked Questions
About LLCs and S Corporations

In this chapter, I will address the critical questions that LLC and S Corporation business owners frequently ask. Understanding these answers is vital for achieving a measure of success in your business endeavors.

What Are the Two Main Types of LLCs?

1. Single Member LLC: This LCC has a single member and is owned and managed by that one person.

2. Multi-member LLC: This LCC has two or more members. A multi-member LLC must decide whether it is going to be member-managed or manager-managed.

   a) A **Member-managed LLC** is when the partners participate in its management. These members must come to a majority agreement before making any major decisions. For example: a loan, a large debt, or purchase.

b) A **Manager-managed LLC** is managed by a specific individual or individuals within the company. A third party who has the authority to make important decisions about the company can also manage it.

CHAPTER 3

What is the Difference Between an S Corporation and an LLC?

An S Corporation (S Corp) and a Limited Liability Company (LLC) are both popular business structures in the United States, each offering unique benefits and drawbacks. Here are the key differences between the two:

1. **Taxation**:
    -   **S Corporation**: An S Corp is a pass-through entity for tax purposes. The business passes through its profits and losses to shareholders, who report them on their personal tax returns. An S Corp submits Form 1120S to the IRS but does not pay federal income tax at the corporate level.

    -   **LLC**: By default, an LLC is also a pass-through entity for tax purposes. Income and losses flow through to members' personal tax returns. However, an LLC can choose to be taxed as a corporation if desired.

2. **Ownership**:
   - **S Corporation**: An S Corp has restrictions on ownership. It cannot have more than one hundred shareholders, and all shareholders must be U.S. citizens or residents.

   - **LLC**: An LLC has more flexibility in ownership. It can have an unlimited number of members. Members can include individuals, corporations, other LLCs, and even foreign entities.

3. **Management**:
   - **S Corporation**: An S Corp has a more structured management system, with a board of directors overseeing major decisions and officers (president, treasurer, etc.) handling day-to-day operations.

   - **LLC**: An LLC offers more flexibility in management structure. Either its members can manage it or appointed managers. This choice allows for more customization based on the needs and preferences of business owners.

4. **Formalities and Compliance**:
   - **S Corporation**: An S Corp has more formalities and compliance requirements than an LLC. This includes holding regular shareholder and director meetings, keeping minutes, and maintaining corporate records.

   - **LLC**: An LLC has fewer formalities and compliance requirements. While it still needs to comply with state regulations, the maintenance requirements are less burdensome than those for an S Corp.

5. **Credibility and Perception**:

- **S Corporation**: Investors and lenders may view an S Corp as more established and credible because of its formal structure and governance requirements.

- **LLC**: An LLC is more flexible and easier to manage, making them attractive for small businesses and startups. However, some investors and lenders may prefer dealing with corporations.

6. **Flexibility in Profit Distribution**:

- **S Corporation**: An S Corp has limitations on profit distribution. Shareholders must receive profits based on their ownership percentage.

- **LLC**: An LLC offers more flexibility in profit distribution. Members can agree on any distribution arrangement they see fit, regardless of their ownership percentage.

Ultimately, the choice between an S Corporation and an LLC depends on various factors, such as taxation preferences, ownership structure, management style, compliance obligations, and long-term business goals. It's advisable to consult with legal and financial professionals to determine the best option for your specific situation.

CHAPTER 4

Can I Save Money By Forming an LLC in a Jurisdiction like Nevada?

While other states do not impose state income tax on an LLC, you are still required to pay federal income tax on your net revenue generated by your LLC.

If you conduct business in other states, you must register your business and fulfill the obligations, such as paying any fees or taxes required for that state.

You can establish a presence in a state through activities such as:

1. Owning property,
2. Conducting business,
3. Maintaining a bank account,
4. Holding meetings, or
5. Selling goods or services.

Should you form your LLC in a state other than the state you live in, I suggest you speak to a tax specialist.

CHAPTER 5

What is the Difference Between a
C Coporation and an S Corporation?

The C Corporation is the standard (or default) corporation under IRS rules. The S Corporation is a corporation that has elected a special tax status with the IRS and therefore has some tax advantages.

Both business structures derive their names from parts of the Internal Revenue Code that govern their taxation. Subchapter C of the Internal Revenue Code taxes C Corporations, while Subchapter S of the Internal Revenue Code taxes S Corporations. To elect S Corporation status when forming a corporation, you must file Form 2553 with the IRS and ensure all S Corporation guidelines are met.

Below are qualities shared by both C Corporations and S Corporations:

Limited liability protection: Corporations offer limited liability protection, so shareholders (owners) are not personally responsible for business debts and liabilities. This is true whether taxed as a C Corporation or an S Corporation. Separate legal entities—corporations (C Corps and S Corps)—are separate legal entities created by a state filing.

Formation documents: You must file formation documents with the state. These documents, which are called the Articles of Incorporation or Certificate of Incorporation, are the same regardless of whether you choose to be taxed as an S Corporation or C Corporation.

Structure: S Corps and C Corps have shareholders, directors, and officers. Shareholders are the owners of the corporation, but it is the corporation that owns the business. Shareholders elect the board of directors. The board oversees and directs the corporation's affairs and decision-making, but is not responsible for day-to-day operations. The board elects officers to manage daily business affairs.

Corporate formalities: The state corporation laws make no distinction between C Corporations and S Corporations with compliance responsibilities. All corporations are required to follow the internal and external corporate formalities and obligations, such as adopting bylaws, issuing stock, holding shareholder and director meetings, maintaining a registered agent and registered office, filing annual reports, and paying annual fees.

CHAPTER 6

S Corporation Versus C Corporation: the Differences

For small business owners evaluating S Corporations versus C Corporations, the decision comes down to how they want the corporation to be treated for federal income tax purposes.

C Corporations: C Corps are separate taxable entities. Owners file a corporate tax return (Form 1120) and pay taxes at the corporate level. Business owners also face the possibility of double taxation if they receive corporate income as dividends, as dividends are considered personal taxable income. Businesses first pay corporate income tax at the corporate level and then face additional taxation at the individual level on dividends.

S Corporations: S Corps are pass-through taxation entities. Owners file an informational federal return (Form 1120S) but pay no income tax at the corporate level. The profits/losses of the business are instead "passed-through" to the business and reported on the owners' personal tax returns. The owners pay any taxes due at the individual level.

Personal income taxes: With both C Corporations and S Corporations, personal income tax is due both on any salary drawn from the corporation and from any dividends received from the corporation.

CHAPTER 7

Corporate Ownership

As we mentioned, state corporation laws make no distinction between S Corporations and C Corporations, but the Internal Revenue Code places several restrictions on who can be shareholders in order for the corporation to qualify to be an S Corp.

Shareholder restrictions: Shareholder restrictions state that S Corps can have no more than 100 shareholders, and shareholders must be U.S. citizens/residents. C Corporations have no restrictions on ownership.

Ownership: S Corporations cannot be owned by C Corporations, other S Corporations (with some exceptions), LLCs, partnerships, or trusts.

Stock: S Corporations can have only one class of stock (disregarding voting rights), while C Corporations can have multiple classes.

CHAPTER 8

Advantages and Disadvantages of
C Corporations and S Corporations

When it comes to structuring a business in the United States, choosing between a C Corporation and an S Corporation is a pivotal decision that can have far-reaching implications. Each entity offers distinct advantages and disadvantages, influencing factors such as taxation, shareholder structure, and business operations. Understanding the nuanced differences between these two types of corporations is essential for business owners and entrepreneurs aiming to optimize their organizational strategy and ensure compliance with federal and state regulations.

S Corporation Advantages

Single layer of taxation: The main advantage of the S Corporation over the C Corporation is that an S Corporation does not pay a corporate-level income tax. So, any distribution of income to shareholders is only taxed at the individual level.

20% qualified business income deduction: The Tax Cuts and Jobs Act of 2017 gave eligible S Corporation shareholders a deduction of up to 20% of net "qualified business income."

Pass-through of losses: The losses of an S Corporation is passed-through to its shareholders, who can use the losses to offset income (subject to restrictions of the tax law).

C Corporation Disadvantages

Limited number of shareholders: An S Corporation cannot have more than 100 shareholders, meaning it can't go public and limits its ability to raise capital from new investors.

Other shareholder restrictions: Shareholders must be individuals (with a few exceptions) and U.S. citizens or residents. This also makes it harder for an S Corporation to obtain equity financing, particularly because venture capital and private equity funds tend to be ineligible shareholders.

Preferred stock not allowed: To be eligible for S Corporation status the corporation cannot have different classes of stock. Some investors want preferences to distributions or other privileges. An S Corporation cannot provide that.

Transfer restrictions: Most S Corps will restrict their shareholders' ability to sell or transfer their shares. That's to make sure they don't end up with an ineligible shareholder which will cause the IRS to terminate its S Corporation status. This makes it harder for the shareholders of an S Corporation to exit the corporation.

C Corporation Advantages

- Unlimited number of shareholders
- There is no limit on the number of shareholders a corporation taxed under Subchapter C can have.
- No restrictions on ownership
- Anyone can own shares, including business entities and non-U.S. citizens.
- No restrictions on classes
- A C Corporation can issue more than one class of stock, including stock with preferences to dividends and distributions.

CHAPTER 9

What is the Start Up Cost to Form an LLC?

There is a cost to form a Limited Liability Company (LLC), and the exact amount varies depending on the state where you are forming the LLC. Here are some common costs associated with forming an LLC:

1. **Filing Fees**: This is the primary cost and varies by state. It ranges from $50 to $500. For example, in California, the fee is $70, while in Massachusetts, it is $500.

2. **Annual/Biennial Fees**: Many states require LLCs to pay an annual or biennial fee to remain in good standing. This can range from $10 to several hundred dollars.

3. **Registered Agent Fees**: If you hire a registered agent service to receive legal documents on behalf of your LLC, it costs between $50 and $300 per year.

4. **Publication Fees**: In some states, such as New York and Arizona, you are required to publish a notice of your LLC

formation in local newspapers, which can cost anywhere from $50 to $2000 depending on the publication and region.

5. **Operating Agreement**: While not always required by law, an operating agreement is advisable. You can draft this yourself or hire a lawyer which can cost a few hundred dollars.

6. **Additional Costs**: These can include business licenses, permits, and other state-specific requirements which may have associated fees.

Online legal services that help with LLC formation also charge a fee, ranging from $50 to $500, including the state filing fees.

It's important to check with your specific state's Secretary of State.

CHAPTER 10

How to Renew Your LLC

In California, an LLC must fulfill specific annual requirements to remain in good standing. These requirements include filing an Annual Report (also known as a Statement of Information) and paying an annual tax. Here are the steps and details for renewing an LLC each year in California:

1. **File the Statement of Information**

    You must file the Statement of Information with the California Secretary of State. Here's how you can do it:

    Frequency: You must file the Statement of Information within 90 days of forming your LLC and then every two years. However, opting to update the information annually keeps your records current.

    Method:
    - **Online**: You can file online through the California Secretary of State's website.

- **Mail**: You can download the form (LLC-12) from the Secretary of State's website, fill it out, and mail it in.

- **In Person**: You can also deliver it in person to the Secretary of State's office.

Information Needed:

- LLC name and Secretary of State file number.

- Principal business address.

- Mailing address, if different.

- Name and address of the agent for service of process.

- Names and addresses of the LLC's manager(s) or member(s).

Fee: The filing fee for the Statement of Information is $20.

2. **Pay the Annual Franchise Tax**

Every LLC registered in California must pay an annual minimum franchise tax to the California Franchise Tax Board (FTB).

Amount: The minimum annual franchise tax is $800.

Due Date: The tax is due by the 15th day of the 4th month after the beginning of the LLC's tax year. For most LLCs, this is April 15th.

Method:

- **Online**: You can make payment through the FTB's website.

- **Mail**: You can send a check or money order along with Form 3522 (LLC Tax Voucher) to the FTB.

3. **File the Annual LLC Fee (if applicable)**

   If your LLC's income exceeds a certain threshold, you may need to pay an additional fee.

   Calculation: This fee is based on the LLC's total income from California sources, not just net income.

   Due Date: The fee is due by the 15th day of the 6th month of the LLC's tax year.

   Method: File Form 3536 (Estimated Fee for LLCs) with the FTB.

Additional Considerations

- **Operating Agreement**: While not required to be filed with the state, keeping an up-to-date operating agreement is crucial for internal governance and record-keeping.

- **Federal Taxes**: Don't forget to file your federal taxes with the IRS. LLCs are typically taxed as pass-through entities, but you may choose to be taxed as a corporation.

Summary of Steps

1. **File the Statement of Information**: Every two years (or annually if preferred) with the California Secretary of State.

2. **Pay the Annual Franchise Tax**: $800 minimum, due by the 15th day of the 4th month of the tax year.

3. **File the Annual LLC Fee**: If applicable, based on the LLC's income, due by the 15th day of the 6th month of the tax year.

By following these steps, your LLC will remain in compliance with California state requirements. For the most current information and forms, visit the California Secretary of State's website and the California Franchise Tax Board's website.

CHAPTER 11

What is the New Business Ownership Information Report?

Beginning January 1, 2024, most small entities, including single member LLCs, must file an online report with the federal government, disclosing information about the beneficial owners of the entities. This was created by the Corporation Transparency Act (CTA).

Existing entities will have until January 1, 2025, to make their first beneficiary ownership information (BOI) report. Entities created or registered in 2024 will have 90 days from creation to get their first reports filed. Any entity that has already filed a report will generally have 30 days to make updates required by the CTA.

Entity type that must file:

1. LLC
2. SMLLC
3. Limited Partnership
4. S Corporation
5. C Corporation
6. Sole Proprietorship (not unless Corporation or LLC)

Should my company report beneficial ownership information now?

FinCEN launched the BOI E-Filing website for reporting beneficial ownership information (https://boiefiling.fincen.gov) on January 1, 2024.

- A reporting company created or registered to do business before January 1, 2024, will have until January 1, 2025, to file its initial BOI report.

- A reporting company created or registered in 2024 will have 90 calendar days to file after receiving actual or public notice that its creation or registration is effective.

- A reporting company created or registered on or after January 1, 2025, will have 30 calendar days to file after receiving actual or public notice that its creation or registration is effective.

When do I need to report my company's beneficial ownership information to FinCEN?

A reporting company created or registered to do business before January 1, 2024, will have until January 1, 2025, to file its initial beneficial ownership information report.

A reporting company created or registered on or after January 1, 2024, and before January 1, 2025, will have 90 calendar days after receiving notice of the company's creation or registration to file its initial BOI report. This 90-calendar day deadline runs from the time the company receives actual notice that its creation or registration is effective, or after a secretary of state or similar office first provides public notice of its creation or registration, whichever is earlier.

Reporting companies created or registered on or after January 1, 2025, will have 30 calendar days from actual or public notice that the company's creation or registration is effective to file their initial BOI reports with FinCEN.

When will FinCEN accept beneficial ownership information reports?

FinCEN will begin accepting beneficial ownership information reports on January 1, 2024. Beneficial ownership information reports will not be accepted before that time.

How will I report my company's beneficial ownership information?

If you are required to report your company's beneficial ownership information to FinCEN, you will do so electronically through a secure filing system available via FinCEN's BO1 E-Filing website (https://boiefiling.fincen.gov).

What happens if a reporting company does not report beneficial ownership information to FinCEN or fails to update or correct the information within the required timeframe?

FinCEN is working hard to ensure that reporting companies are aware of their obligations to report, update, and correct beneficial ownership information. FinCEN understands this is a new requirement. If you correct a mistake or omission within 90 days of the deadline for the original report, you may avoid being penalized. However, you could face civil and criminal penalties if you disregard your beneficial ownership information reporting obligations.

FinCEN's Small Entity Compliance Guide provides more information about enforcement of the requirement (see Chapter 1.3, "What happens if my company does not report BOI in the required timeframe?").

What penalties do individuals face for violating BOI reporting requirements?

As specified in the Corporate Transparency Act, a person who willfully violates the BOI reporting requirements may be subject to civil penalties of up to **$500 for each day** that the violation continues. That person may also be subject to criminal penalties of **up to two years imprisonment and a fine of up to $10,000.** Potential violations include willfully failing to file a beneficial ownership information report, willfully filing false beneficial ownership information, or willfully failing to correct or update previously reported beneficial ownership information.

CHAPTER 12

What is the Difference Between S Corporation and LLC Taxation?

S Corporations (S Corps) and Limited Liability Companies (LLCs) are both popular business structures in the United States, each offering unique benefits and drawbacks. Here are the key differences between the two:

1. **Taxation**:
   - **S Corporation**: S Corps are pass-through entities for tax purposes, meaning the profits and losses of the business are passed through to the shareholders and reported on their personal tax returns. S Corps file Form 1120S with the IRS, but they don't pay federal income tax at the corporate level.

   - **LLC**: By default, LLCs are also pass-through entities for tax purposes. Income and losses flow through to members' personal tax returns. However, an LLC can choose to be taxed as a corporation if desired.

2. **Ownership**:
   - **S Corporation**: S Corps have restrictions on ownership. They cannot have more than 100 shareholders, and all shareholders must be U.S. citizens or residents.

   - **LLC**: LLCs have more flexibility in ownership. They can have an unlimited number of members, and members can include individuals, corporations, other LLCs, and even foreign entities.

3. **Management**:
   - **S Corporation**: S Corps have a more structured management system, with a board of directors overseeing major decisions and officers (president, treasurer, etc.) handling day-to-day operations.

   - **LLC**: LLCs offer more flexibility in management structure. They can be managed either by their members or by appointed managers. This choice allows for more customization based on the needs and preferences of business owners.

4. **Formalities and Compliance**:
   - **S Corporation**: S Corps generally have more formalities and compliance requirements than an LLCs. This includes holding regular shareholder and director meetings, keeping minutes, and maintaining corporate records.

   - **LLC**: LLCs have fewer formalities and compliance requirements. While they still need to comply with state regulations, maintenance requirements are generally less burdensome than those for S Corps.

5. **Credibility and Perception**:
   - **S Corporation**: S Corps may be perceived as more established and credible by investors and lenders due to their formal structure and governance requirements.

   - **LLC**: LLCs are often seen as more flexible and easier to manage, making them attractive for small businesses and startups. However, some investors and lenders may prefer dealing with corporations.

6. **Flexibility in Profit Distribution**:
   - **S Corporation**: S Corps have limitations on profit distribution. Profits must be distributed to shareholders based on their ownership percentage.

   - **LLC**: LLCs offer more flexibility in profit distribution. Members can agree on any distribution arrangement they see fit, regardless of their ownership percentage.

Ultimately, the choice between an S Corporation and an LLC depends on various factors such as taxation preferences, ownership structure, management style, compliance obligations, and long-term business goals. It's advisable to consult with legal and financial professionals to determine the best option for your specific situation.

CHAPTER 13

Is the Tax Rate for a C Corporation Higher
Than That for an S Corporation?

The tax rate for a regular corporation (C Corporation) is different from that of an S Corporation. Here's how they compare:

1. **C Corporation**:
    *   C Corporations are subject to corporate income tax at the federal level. As of my last update, the corporate tax rate under the Tax Cuts and Jobs Act of 2017 (TCJA) was a flat rate of 21% on taxable income. This rate applies to C Corporations' profits before any distributions to shareholders.

2. **S Corporation**:
    *   S Corporations are pass-through entities for tax purposes. This means that the corporation itself does not pay federal income tax on its profits. Instead, the profits and losses "pass through" to shareholders, who report them on their individual tax returns. Shareholders then pay taxes on their share of the S Corporation's income at their individual tax rates.

- The tax treatment of S Corporations can result in potentially lower overall taxes for shareholders compared to C Corporations, especially for smaller businesses.

It's important to note that while S Corporations offer potential tax advantages, they have certain eligibility requirements and restrictions, such as the limitation on the number and type of shareholders (e.g., individuals, certain trusts, and estates) and the requirement that all shareholders must be U.S. citizens or residents.

Before choosing between a C Corporation and an S Corporation, it's crucial to consider various factors such as the business's financial situation, long-term goals, ownership structure, and tax implications. Consulting with a tax advisor or accountant can provide personalized guidance based on the specific circumstances of the business.

CHAPTER 14

Does an S Corporation Need a Corporate Manual?

An S Corporation, like any other corporation, may find it beneficial to have a corporate manual or handbook, even if it's not selling stock. While not a legal requirement, a corporate manual serves as a valuable tool for organizing and managing the company's operations. Here are some reasons why an S Corp might choose to have a corporate manual:

1. **Clarity and Consistency**: A corporate manual helps ensure that everyone within the organization understands the company's policies, procedures, and expectations. This can lead to more consistent operations and decision-making.

2. **Employee Training**: It serves as a valuable resource for onboarding new employees and training existing ones. A well-documented manual can help employees understand their roles and responsibilities within the company.

3. **Compliance and Risk Management**: A corporate manual can outline compliance requirements, such as workplace safety,

confidentiality, and anti-discrimination policies. It can also provide guidance on handling various situations, reducing the risk of legal issues and liabilities.

4. **Communication Tool**: It fosters effective communication within the company by clearly outlining procedures for internal processes, such as performance evaluations, leave policies, and conflict resolution.

5. **Company Culture and Values**: A corporate manual can reflect the company's culture and values, helping to align employees with the organization's mission and goals.

While an S Corporation may not issue stock in the same way as a traditional corporation, it still operates under corporate governance principles and may benefit from the structure and organization provided by a corporate manual. Ultimately, whether to have a corporate manual depends on the specific needs and goals of the company.

CHAPTER 15

Does a C Corporation Need a Corporate Manual?

There is no legal requirement for C Corporation to have a corporate manual. However, many C Corporations choose to create and maintain corporate manuals or employee handbooks for the following reasons:

1. **Clarity and Consistency**: A corporate manual helps ensure that everyone within the organization understands the company's policies, procedures, and expectations, leading to more consistent operations and decision-making.

2. **Employee Training and Onboarding**: It serves as a valuable resource for new employee orientation and ongoing training. A well-documented manual can help employees understand their roles and responsibilities within the company.

3. **Compliance and Risk Management**: A corporate manual can outline legal and regulatory requirements, as well as internal policies for compliance with laws such as workplace safety, equal employment opportunity, and harassment prevention.

It can also provide guidance on handling various situations, reducing the risk of legal issues and liabilities.

4. **Communication Tool**: It facilitates effective communication within the company by clearly outlining procedures for internal processes, such as performance evaluations, leave policies, and disciplinary actions.

5. **Company Culture and Values**: A corporate manual can reflect the company's culture and values, helping to align employees with the organization's mission and goals.

While a corporate manual is not mandatory for a C Corporation, it can be a valuable tool for promoting consistency, compliance, and communication within the organization. Additionally, having documented policies and procedures may be beneficial in case of legal disputes or regulatory inquiries.

CHAPTER 16

Does an LLC Need a Corporate Manual?

While it's not a legal requirement for an LLC that's not electing S Corp status to have a corporate manual, it can still be a valuable tool for organizing and managing the company. A corporate manual, also known as an operating manual or an operations manual, outlines the policies, procedures, and guidelines for running the business efficiently and effectively.

Even though LLCs have more flexibility and fewer formal requirements than corporations, having a corporate manual can still provide several benefits:

1. **Clarity and Consistency**: It ensures that everyone in the company understands how things are supposed to be done, which can lead to more consistent operations and decision-making.

2. **Training Tool**: Use it as a training resource for new employees, helping them understand the company's processes and expectations.

3. **Risk Management**: A well-documented manual can help mitigate risks by providing guidelines for handling various situations, such as customer complaints, employee conflicts, or legal issues.

4. **Succession Planning**: If the business expands or if key employees leave, having a manual in place can make transitions smoother by providing continuity in operations.

5. **Legal Protection**: While not a substitute for legal advice, a corporate manual can demonstrate that the company has established policies and procedures, which may be beneficial in case of legal disputes.

Ultimately, whether or not to create a corporate manual depends on the specific needs and goals of the LLC. For some small businesses, informal practices may suffice, while others may benefit from the structure and organization provided by a comprehensive manual. It's a decision best made by considering the company's size, complexity, industry, and future plans.

CHAPTER 17

Is an S Corporation Required to Keep Minutes?

While keeping minutes of meetings is not a legal requirement for S Corporations like it is for C Corporations, it's still good practice. Minutes of meetings document the decisions made and actions taken by the shareholders and directors, similar to their role in C Corporations. Though the IRS doesn't specifically require S Corporations to keep minutes, maintaining accurate records of meetings can still be beneficial for several reasons:

1. **Legal Compliance**: Although not mandatory, keeping minutes can demonstrate that the S Corporation is following proper corporate governance procedures, which can be important in legal proceedings or regulatory inquiries.

2. **Record of Decisions**: Minutes provide a written record of decisions made by the shareholders and directors, such as elections of officers, approval of financial statements, and other important matters.

3. **Liability Protection**: Detailed minutes can help protect directors and officers from personal liability by showing that they acted in accordance with their fiduciary duties.

4. **Historical Record**: Minutes serve as a historical record of the S Corporation's activities, which can be valuable for future reference, strategic planning, and maintaining continuity of operations.

5. **Transparency and Accountability**: Maintaining minutes promotes transparency and accountability within the corporation by providing shareholders, regulators, and other stakeholders with insight into the decision-making process.

While S Corporations may not face the same legal consequences for failing to keep minutes as C Corporations do, the benefits of maintaining accurate records often outweigh the effort involved. Additionally, it's essential to consult with legal and financial professionals to ensure compliance with any specific state or federal regulations that may apply to S Corporation record-keeping.

CHAPTER 18

Is a C Corporation Required to Keep Minutes?

A C Corporation is typically required to keep minutes of its meetings of shareholders and directors. Minutes are the official written record of what transpired during these meetings, including decisions made, actions taken, and discussions held.

Keeping accurate minutes is important for several reasons:

1. **Legal Compliance**: Minutes serve as evidence that the corporation is following proper corporate governance procedures, which is essential for legal compliance.

2. **Record of Decisions**: Minutes document the decisions made by the board of directors and shareholders, including approval of important matters such as financial statements, corporate transactions, and changes to bylaws.

3. **Liability Protection**: Detailed minutes can help protect directors and officers from personal liability by demonstrating that they acted in accordance with their fiduciary duties.

4. **Historical Record**: Minutes provide a historical record of the corporation's activities, which can be valuable for future reference, strategic planning, and continuity of operations.

5. **Transparency**: Keeping minutes promotes transparency and accountability within the corporation by providing shareholders, regulators, and other stakeholders with insight into the decision-making process.

While the specific requirements for minutes may vary depending on the jurisdiction and the corporation's bylaws, it's generally advisable for C Corporations to maintain accurate and comprehensive minutes of their meetings. Failure to keep proper minutes could result in legal and regulatory consequences, including fines, penalties, and challenges to corporate decisions.

CHAPTER 19

Can an LLC Issue Stock?

Generally, LLCs cannot issue stock like corporations can. Stock issuance is a feature specific to corporations, where ownership is represented by shares of stock.

However, there are ways an LLC can achieve something similar:

1. **Membership Interest**: Instead of stock, LLCs issue membership interests. These interests represent a share of ownership in the company and entitle the holder to a portion of the LLC's profits and losses, as well as voting rights and other membership rights as defined in the LLC's operating agreement.

2. **Units or Ownership Interests**: LLCs can issue units or ownership interests, which are similar to shares of stock in corporations. These units can be sold or transferred to new members or investors.

3. **Convertible Securities**: An LLC may issue convertible securities, such as convertible debt or convertible preferred interests, which can be converted into membership interests

or units at a later time, typically upon certain conditions or events.

4. **Equity Incentive Plans**: Although not as common as in corporations, LLCs can establish equity incentive plans, such as profit interests or phantom equity, to provide incentives to key employees or consultants. These plans grant the right to receive a share of the LLC's future profits or appreciation in value.

It's important to note that the rules and regulations regarding ownership interests in an LLC vary by jurisdiction, so it's advisable to consult with legal and financial professionals familiar with the laws in the relevant jurisdiction before issuing membership interests or units. Additionally, the LLC's operating agreement will typically outline the procedures for issuing and transferring ownership interests within the company.

CHAPTER 20

What are the Different Kinds of Stocks?

Stocks, representing ownership in a company, come in various forms, each with unique characteristics and purposes. Here are the primary types of stocks:

1. **Common Stock:**

   - **Voting Rights:** Common stockholders typically have voting rights, allowing them to vote on corporate matters, including the election of the board of directors.

   - **Dividends:** Dividends are not guaranteed and can fluctuate based on the company's profitability.

   - **Capital Appreciation:** Common stocks offer the potential for capital appreciation, meaning the value of the stock can increase over time, providing returns through price gains.

2. **Preferred Stock:**

   - **Dividends**: Preferred stockholders usually receive fixed dividends, which are paid out before any dividends to common stockholders.

   - **Priority**: In the event of liquidation, preferred stockholders have a higher claim on assets than common stockholders but are subordinate to debt holders.

   - **Limited Voting Rights**: Preferred stocks generally do not come with voting rights.

3. **Growth Stocks:**

   - **High Growth Potential**: These stocks are from companies expected to grow at an above-average rate compared to other companies.

   - **Reinvestment**: Companies often reinvest earnings into the business rather than paying dividends.

4. **Value Stocks:**

   - **Undervalued**: These stocks are considered undervalued based on financial metrics such as price-to-earnings ratios.

   - **Dividends**: They often pay regular dividends and are perceived as less risky compared to growth stocks.

5. **Blue-Chip Stocks:**

   - **Reputation**: These are stocks of large, well-established, and financially sound companies with a history of reliable performance.

- **Dividends**: They usually pay steady dividends and are considered relatively safe investments.

6. **Income Stocks**:

   - **High Dividends**: Known for paying high and regular dividends, providing a steady income stream to investors.

   - **Stability**: Often found in mature industries with stable earnings.

7. **Cyclical Stocks**:

   - **Economic Sensitivity**: These stocks are closely tied to the economic cycle and tend to perform well during economic expansions and poorly during contractions.

   - **Industries**: Common in industries such as automotive, housing, and luxury goods.

8. **Defensive Stocks**:

   - **Resilience**: These stocks are from companies that provide essential goods and services and tend to perform well during economic downturns.

   - **Industries**: Often found in industries like utilities, healthcare, and consumer staples.

9. **Penny Stocks**:

   - **Low Price**: Typically trade for less than $5 per share and are often associated with small companies.

- **High Risk**: Known for high volatility and risk, with potential for significant gains or losses.

10. Small-Cap, Mid-Cap, and Large-Cap Stocks:

- **Market Capitalization**: These categories are based on the company's market capitalization:

- **Small-Cap**: Companies with market caps between $300 million and $2 billion.

- **Mid-Cap**: Companies with market caps between $2 billion and $10 billion.

- **Large-Cap**: Companies with market caps over $10 billion.

- **Risk and Growth**: Small-cap stocks are often more volatile and offer higher growth potential, while large-cap stocks are generally more stable and less risky.

- **International Stocks: Global Exposure**: Stocks of companies based outside the investor's home country.

- **Diversification**: Provide diversification benefits and exposure to global markets.

11. ESG (Environmental, Social, Governance) Stocks:

- **Sustainability Focus**: Stocks of companies that adhere to environmental, social, and governance criteria.

- **Ethical Investing**: Popular among investors who prioritize ethical and sustainable business practices.

Understanding the different types of stocks can help investors build a diversified portfolio that aligns with their financial goals, risk tolerance, and investment strategy.

CHAPTER 21

What are the Disadvantages of a Single-Member LLC?

While single-member LLCs (Limited Liability Companies) offer numerous benefits, such as simplicity in formation and flexibility in management, they also come with certain disadvantages:

1. **Limited Liability Protection May Be Challenged**:

    *   In some cases, courts may "pierce the corporate veil" if they determine that the LLC is not being operated as a separate entity from its owner. This could expose the owner to personal liability for the business's debts and obligations.

2. **Self-Employment Taxes**:

    *   Single-member LLC owners are considered self-employed and must pay self-employment taxes on their business income. This includes both the employer and employee portions of Social Security and Medicare taxes, which can be a significant expense.

3. **Limited Access to Capital**:

   - Raising capital can be more challenging for single-member LLCs compared to corporations. Investors may be less inclined to invest in an LLC due to the perceived informality and lack of corporate structure.

4. **Less Perceived Credibility**:

   - Some clients, customers, or investors may perceive single-member LLCs as less credible or established than corporations, potentially affecting business opportunities.

5. **Complexity in Record Keeping**:

   - While simpler than corporations, single-member LLCs still require diligent record-keeping and separation of personal and business finances to maintain limited liability protection.

6. **Possible Higher State Fees**:

   - Some states impose higher annual fees or taxes on LLCs compared to other business structures, such as sole proprietorships or partnerships.

7. **Transition and Succession Issues**:

   - In the event of the owner's death or incapacitation, transferring ownership can be more complicated compared to a corporation with a more clearly defined structure for succession.

8. Lack of Continuity:

- Single-member LLCs might face dissolution upon the death or withdrawal of the sole member unless otherwise stated in the operating agreement, leading to potential business disruptions.

Understanding these disadvantages can help in making an informed decision about whether a single-member LLC is the right business structure for your needs.

CHAPTER 22

What are the Disadvantages of Putting Your House or Apartment in an LLC?

Putting your house or apartment in a Limited Liability Company (LLC) can have several disadvantages, depending on your specific circumstances and goals:

1. **Complexity and Costs**: Establishing and maintaining an LLC involves paperwork, legal fees, and ongoing administrative tasks, such as filing annual reports and paying state fees. These expenses can add up over time.

2. **Tax Implications**: While an LLC can offer certain tax advantages, such as pass-through taxation, it can also have drawbacks. Depending on the structure of the LLC and its income, you may face higher taxes compared to owning the property personally. Additionally, transferring ownership of the property to an LLC may trigger tax consequences, such as a capital gains tax.

3. **Lender Restrictions**: If you have a mortgage on the property, transferring ownership to an LLC might violate the terms of

your loan agreement. Many mortgage lenders include a due-on-sale clause, which allows them to demand full repayment of the loan if the property ownership changes. You may need to seek permission from your lender before transferring ownership to an LLC.

4. **Personal Liability**: While the primary purpose of an LLC is to limit personal liability, there are situations where you could still be personally liable. For example, if you personally guarantee the LLC's debts or liabilities, or if you commingle personal and business finances, you may lose the liability protection offered by the LLC.

5. **Difficulty Obtaining Financing**: It might be more challenging to secure financing for properties held within an LLC, especially if the LLC has a limited financial history or if lenders are unfamiliar with the structure.

6. **Reduced Privacy**: LLC ownership is a matter of public record, so transferring your property to an LLC could result in reduced privacy regarding your ownership interests.

7. **Potential Transfer Issues**: Selling or transferring ownership of a property held within an LLC can be more complicated than selling a property owned personally. Buyers may be hesitant to purchase a property held within an LLC due to concerns about assuming the LLC's liabilities or complications related to the transfer process.

Before transferring your property to an LLC, it's essential to consult with legal, tax, and financial professionals to fully understand the implications and determine if it's the right decision for your situation.

CHAPTER 23

Is an LLC Subject to Taxation?

An LLC is considered a Taxable entity for all tax purposes.

1. An LLC itself is not subject to taxation.

2. An LLC tax depends on the number of members it has.

3. A Single-member LLC is taxed as a sole proprietorship, whereas the income is reported on the owner's personal taxes return using Schedule C.

4. A multi-member LLC is subject to a partnership taxation, where the partnership files an information return (Form 1065) and issues Schedule K-1 to each partner, reflecting their share of the earnings to be reported on their individual tax return.

5. An LLC can choose to be taxed as a corporation.

CHAPTER 24

Can an LLC Have Multiple Business Ventures?

An LLC (Limited Liability Company) can have multiple business ventures operating under its umbrella. This is often done for simplicity in management and administration, as well as for liability protection purposes. Instead of creating a separate LLC for each business venture, which would require separate filings, fees, and administrative tasks, multiple ventures can be managed under one LLC.

Each business activity can be structured as a separate division or operating entity within the LLC. This allows the LLC to engage in various activities while maintaining a centralized structure for management, finances, and legal liability. However, it's important to ensure that the LLC's operating agreement and any necessary legal documents clearly outline the rights, responsibilities, and relationships between each business activity within the LLC.

Additionally, it's advisable to consult with legal and financial professionals to ensure compliance with applicable laws and regulations, as well as to address any specific considerations related to structuring multiple businesses under one LLC.

CHAPTER 25

Can an LLC Member Be Held Personally Liable For the Debts of the LLC?

Generally, members of an LLC are not personally liable for the debts and obligations of the LLC. One of the primary benefits of forming an LLC is that it provides limited liability protection to its members. This means that the personal assets of the members (such as their personal bank accounts, homes, and cars) are typically protected from being used to satisfy the debts and liabilities of the LLC. However, there are several exceptions where members can be held personally liable:

Personal Guarantees: If a member personally guarantees a loan or other obligation of the LLC, they can be held personally liable if the LLC defaults on that obligation.

Piercing the Corporate Veil: Courts may "pierce the corporate veil" and hold members personally liable if the LLC is found to be a sham or if the members have not maintained the LLC as a separate entity. Factors that can lead to this include commingling personal and business funds, undercapitalization, failing to follow corporate formalities, or committing fraud.

Fraud and Illegal Activities: Members can be personally liable for their own wrongful actions, such as fraud, illegal activities, or negligent conduct that causes harm to others.

Unpaid Employment Taxes: In some cases, members may be held personally liable for certain unpaid taxes, such as employment taxes.

Professional Liability: If the LLC provides professional services (such as legal or medical services), the professionals providing those services may be personally liable for malpractice or other professional misconduct.

It's important for LLC members to adhere to good business practices, maintain proper records, and keep personal and business finances separate to maintain their limited liability protection. Consulting with legal and financial professionals can help ensure that members understand their responsibilities and the best practices for protecting their personal liability.

CHAPTER 26

Can an LLC Have Multiple LLC Businesses?

An LLC (Limited Liability Company) can have multiple business ventures or operations under a single LLC entity. This is commonly done through the creation of "series" or "subsidiaries" within the primary LLC. Here are a few ways to structure this:

1. **Single LLC with Multiple DBAs (Doing Business As):**
   The primary LLC can operate multiple businesses under different names by registering DBAs for each separate business. This keeps all operations under the same legal entity while allowing each business to have its own identity.

2. **Series LLC:**
   Some states allow for the formation of a Series LLC, which is a single LLC with multiple "series" or "cells" that operate independently of each other. Each series can have its own assets, members, and operations, providing a layer of liability protection among the series.

3. **Holding Company with Subsidiaries:**
   The primary LLC Can act as a holding company that owns several subsidiary LLCs. Each subsidiary operates a different business. This structure provides liability protection for each business and can help with organization and management.

4. **Legal and Financial Liability:**
   While a single LLC with multiple DBAs is simpler and less costly to maintain, it does not provide separate liability protection for each business. In contrast, a Series LLC or a holding company with subsidiaries can provide distinct liability protection for each business.

5. **State Regulations:**
   The availability and rules regarding Series LLCs and the use of DBAs vary by state. It's important to check with your state's specific regulations regarding these structures.

6. **Tax Implications:**
   Each structure can have different tax implications. It's advisable to consult with a tax professional to understand the tax responsibilities for each type of structure.

7. **Administrative Complexity:**
   Managing multiple businesses under one LLC can become administratively complex, especially if they are distinct. Proper bookkeeping and accounting practices are essential to keep the operations separate and organized.

Example Scenario:

You own ABC Ventures LLC. Under this LLC, you want to run three different businesses: a coffee shop, a web development agency, and a real estate rental service. You could structure it as follows:

1. **Single LLC with DBAs:**
    ABC Ventures LLC operates as "ABC Coffee Shop," "ABC Web Development," and "ABC Rentals," with each business registered as a DBA.

2. **Series LLC (if your state allows):**
    ABC Ventures LLC Creates Series A for the coffee shop, Series B for the web development agency, and Series C for the real estate rental service. Each series operates independently, with separate assets and liabilities.

3. **Holding Company Structure:**
    ABC Ventures LLC (the holding company) forms three separate LLCs: "ABC Coffee LLC," "ABC Web Development LLC," and "ABC Rentals LLC." Each subsidiary operates its respective business.

Each structure has its advantages and disadvantages, and the best choice depends on your specific business needs, liability concerns, and administrative capacity. One concern would be that a lawsuit filed against one of the businesses could put the assets of the other businesses at risk. Consulting with a legal or business advisor can help determine the most suitable structure for your situation.

CHAPTER 27

How Do You Dissolve an LLC?

Dissolving a Limited Liability Company (LLC) involves several steps, which can vary depending on the state in which the LLC is registered. However, there are common steps that most LLCs will follow:

1. **Member Approval:**
   Obtain agreement from all members of the LLC to dissolve the company. This may require a formal vote or written consent, depending on the operating agreement.

2. **Review Governing Documents and State Laws:**
   Check the LLC's operating agreement and state laws to ensure compliance with any specific procedures or requirements for dissolution.

3. **File Articles of Dissolution:**
   Submit the necessary dissolution forms (often called "Articles of Dissolution" or "Certificate of Dissolution") with the state's Secretary of State or equivalent agency. There is usually a fee for filing these forms.

4. **Notify Creditors and Settle Debts:**

   Inform all creditors and settle any outstanding debts or obligations. This step might involve sending a formal notice to creditors and paying off any liabilities.

5. **Liquidate Assets:**

   Sell off the LLC's assets and distribute the proceeds to the members according to their ownership interests and any agreements in place.

6. **File Final Tax Returns:**

   File the final federal, state, and local tax returns, and pay any remaining taxes. Inform the IRS and state tax authorities that the LLC is being dissolved.

7. **Cancel Permits, Licenses, and Business Names:**

   Cancel any business permits or licenses associated with the LLC and withdraw any business name registrations.

8. **Maintain Records:**

   Keep detailed records of the dissolution process and any final transactions for a specified period as required by law.

Detailed Steps

1. **Member Approval:**

   Hold a meeting if required and record the decision in the meeting minutes or through a written consent form.

2. **Articles of Dissolution:**

   Obtain the appropriate form from the state's business filing office.

Complete and submit it along with the required fee. For example, in California, this form is filed with the Secretary of State.

3. **Notify Creditors:**
   Prepare a letter to notify all creditors of the LLC's dissolution and provide them with instructions for submitting claims.

4. **Liquidate Assets:**
   Sell the LLC's assets and convert them to cash. If there are physical assets, this might involve holding a sale or auction.

5. **Distribute Remaining Assets:**
   After paying off debts, distribute any remaining assets to members in accordance with the operating agreement or state law.

6. **File Final Tax Returns:**
   Close the LLC's Employer Identification Number (EIN) account with the IRS if applicable. File final state and federal tax returns and pay any outstanding taxes.

7. **Cancel Registrations:**
   Cancel business licenses, permits, and any registered trade names or DBAs.

8. **Record Keeping:**
   Store all documents related to the dissolution, including minutes of meetings, consent forms, tax returns, and notices to creditors.

Example Process for California:

1. **Member Approval:** Obtain consent from all members as per the operating agreement.

2. **Articles of Dissolution:** File Form LLC-3 (Certificate of Dissolution) and Form LLC-4/7 (Certificate of Cancellation).

3. **Notify Creditors:** Send written notices to creditors.

4. **Liquidate Assets:** Sell assets and settle debts.

5. **Distribute Assets:** Follow the operating agreement for distributing remaining assets.

6. **Final Tax Returns:** File final tax returns and pay all taxes.

7. **Cancel Registrations:** Cancel any business permits and the LLC's EIN with the IRS.

8. **Maintain Records:** Keep all dissolution documents for future reference.

Always consult with a legal professional or accountant to ensure that all legal and financial obligations are properly addressed.

CHAPTER 28

How Do You Dissolve an S Corporation?

Dissolving an S Corporation involves several steps, which can vary depending on the state in which the corporation is registered. Below are the general steps required:

Steps to Dissolve an S Corporation

1. **Shareholder Approval:**
   Obtain approval from the shareholders to dissolve the corporation. This typically requires a vote and adherence to the procedures outlined in the corporation's bylaws.

2. **File Articles of Dissolution:**
   File the necessary dissolution forms, often called "Articles of Dissolution" or "Certificate of Dissolution," with the state's Secretary of State or equivalent agency. There is usually a fee for this filing.

3. **Notify Creditors and Settle Debts:**
   Inform all creditors of the dissolution and settle any outstanding debts and obligations. This might involve sending formal notices to creditors.

4. **Liquidate Assets:**

   Sell the corporation's assets and distribute the proceeds to pay off debts. Any remaining assets should be distributed to the shareholders according to their ownership percentages.

5. **File Final Tax Returns:**

   File the final federal, state, and local tax returns, and pay any remaining taxes. Inform the IRS and state tax authorities that the corporation is being dissolved.

6. **Cancel Permits, Licenses, and Business Names:**

   Cancel any business permits or licenses associated with the corporation and withdraw any business name registrations.

7. **Maintain Records:**

   Keep detailed records of the dissolution process and any final transactions for a specified period as required by law.

Detailed Steps

1. **Shareholder Approval:**

   Hold a formal meeting to vote on the dissolution. Ensure the decision is recorded in the meeting minutes or through a written consent form, adhering to the corporation's bylaws and state laws.

2. **File Articles of Dissolution:**

   Obtain the necessary form from the state's business filing office. Complete and submit it along with the required fee. For example, in California, you would file Form DISS STK (Certificate of Dissolution) and Form DISS NP (Certificate of Election to Wind Up and Dissolve) if applicable.

3. **Notify Creditors:**

   Prepare and send a letter to notify all creditors of the corporation's dissolution. Provide instructions for submitting claims and ensure all debts are settled.

4. **Liquidate Assets:**

   Convert the corporation's assets into cash by selling them. If there are physical assets, this might involve holding a sale or auction. Use the proceeds to pay off any remaining debts.

5. **Distribute Remaining Assets:**

   After settling debts, distribute any remaining assets to shareholders in accordance with their ownership interests and the corporation's bylaws.

6. **File Final Tax Returns:**

   File the final federal, state, and local tax returns, including IRS Form 1120S (U.S. Income Tax Return for an S Corporation). Pay any remaining taxes and inform the IRS of the dissolution. You may need to check the box indicating that it is the final return.

7. **Cancel Registrations:**

   Cancel business licenses, permits, and any registered trade names or DBAs. Close the corporation's Employer Identification Number (EIN) account with the IRS if applicable.

8. **Record Keeping:**
   Maintain all documents related to the dissolution, such as minutes of meetings, consent forms, tax returns, and notices to creditors, for a period specified by state law or best practices (usually several years).

Example Process for California:

1. **Shareholder Approval**: Hold a meeting, vote on dissolution, and record the decision in the minutes.

2. **Articles of Dissolution:** File Form DISS STK with the California Secretary of State.

3. **Notify Creditors:** Send written notices to creditors and settle any debts.

4. **Liquidate Assets:** Sell assets and use proceeds to pay off debts

5. **Distribute Assets:** Distribute any remaining assets to shareholders as per their ownership interests.

6. **Final Tax Returns:** File final tax returns with the IRS and California Franchise Tax Board, paying any remaining taxes.

7. **Cancel Registrations:** Cancel business permits and close the corporation's EIN with the IRS.

8. **Maintain Records:** Keep all dissolution-related documents for future reference.

Always consult with a legal professional or accountant to ensure that all legal and financial obligations are properly addressed and to navigate any specific state requirements.

CONCLUSION

The more you learn, the more you can earn. The more you earn, the more you can pass down to the next generation, creating generational wealth.

The business world has drastically changed. Doing business in a digital space and in the AI (Artificial Intelligence) technology era means there is no more business as usual. The business landscape has changed. Do not lag with technology and know that both digital technology and AI are here to stay.

Laws, regulations, and business requirements are different in many states. I recommend you check the laws and regulations of the state in which you choose to do business. Check with your city and state regarding laws and regulations that govern the operation of LLCs. Check with the IRS regarding federal law that governs LLCs and S Corporations.

There are several books written on starting and managing LLCs. There is also much information you can gather from the Internet that is helpful. It is a great idea to seek a mentor for your business. It's critical to fail proof your business. Arm yourself by seeking the information needed to get started in a no trial-and-error fashion.

I started My Tech Academy to equip entrepreneurs with the knowledge needed to succeed in the world of technology and AI.

I wish you success in your business endeavors.

www.ingramcontent.com/pod-product-compliance
Lightning Source LLC
Chambersburg PA
CBHW031952190326
41519CB00007B/773